How to Recover from the Heartbreak of Pet Loss

How to Recover from the Heartbreak of Pet Loss

Steven H. Woodward

XULON PRESS

Xulon Press
2301 Lucien Way #415
Maitland, FL 32751
407.339.4217
www.xulonpress.com

© 2019 by Steven H. Woodward

All rights reserved solely by the author. The author guarantees all contents are original and do not infringe upon the legal rights of any other person or work. No part of this book may be reproduced in any form without the permission of the author. The views expressed in this book are not necessarily those of the publisher.

Unless otherwise indicated, Scripture quotations taken from the King James Version (KJV)–*public domain*.

Printed in the United States of America.

ISBN-13: 978-1-54567-154-2

TABLE OF CONTENTS

Introduction to Pet Loss ix

Chapter One:	Proof of the Soul and the Afterlife 1	
Chapter Two:	Losing a Beloved Pet 7	
Chapter Three:	Science and the Bible Prove That Animals Have Souls 13	
Chapter Four:	Science and the Bible Prove That Animals are Capable of Thinking and Reasoning 19	
Chapter Five:	Science and the Bible Prove That Animals Have Feelings. 25	
Chapter Six:	Visions of Heaven and Near Death Experiences 27	
Chapter Seven:	Why Do I Grieve?. 35	
Chapter Eight:	Am I Crazy for Grieving over My Animal? . 39	
Chapter Nine:	How Do I Recover from My Loss?. 45	
Chapter Ten:	True Stories of Animals that Saved People . . 55	
Chapter Eleven:	True Stories of People Who Have Seen Their Animals in Heaven 63	

Chapter Twelve: My Trip to Heaven: What I
                 Learned about the Soul 69

A Ten-Step Program To Recovery 75

About the Author 79

Works Cited 85

Prologue

In my first book I recount my divine experience where I was taken to Heaven in a vision to see my beloved dog BJ. In this book I have expounded on the Spiritual, and the Afterlife knowledge that was given to me while in Heaven, in hopes of bringing comfort to those who have loved and lost a beloved animal. I also present both Scientific and Biblical proof which surprisingly, agrees with each other on many issues concerning death, the soul, and the afterlife. This book will help you through the grief process and into a healthy recovery. I have also included a Ten-Step Recovery Program that will guide and help you in your loss. After reading this book you will know the real truth about animals, their souls, and the afterlife. Knowing these truths will turn your grief into hope and joy. This book will heal you and Bless you.
S.W.

Introduction To Pet Loss

Many of us have lost a beloved pet and we know the pain that is associated with it and we want to know, *"Is there an afterlife for animals too? Will I see my pet again? Will my deceased pet be mad or jealous if I adopt again?"* We grieve for our animals as if they were human, and we want to know why we grieve so much over an animal, and why many people don't understand our grief over an animal.

Pet loss grief is a real emotion, make no mistake about it. It is Scientifically proven that pet loss affects us mentally, physically, and spiritually. The reason for this is because we have a special unconditional love for animals that many people do not have; nor do they understand. We have an unconditional love for our pets, and we see ourselves in our animals. They comfort us, they love us unconditionally, and they complete our family. When we adopt an animal, it becomes part of the family and that animal brings love to all the family members and when it passes, we grieve just as though we had lost a human family member.

We unlike non-animal lovers, can see and feel the spirits and souls of our animals. We know that they are *sentient beings* with souls and spirits, because our souls connect with their souls. We can bond with the soul of our animal and when we lose a beloved animal, our souls are temporarily separated, and this is what causes the pain. I will explain what causes this pain and how to deal with it. However, the good news is that our souls are not separated permanently or disconnected forever and that we will see them again. I intend to prove this using both Science and the Bible.

Chapter One

PROOF OF THE SOUL AND THE AFTERLIFE

Spirits and souls are energy and Scientists have proven beyond a shadow of a doubt, that energy never dissipates or dies; it only transfers somewhere else. *But where?* Some people believe that the soul of their animal goes to Heaven and some believe that the soul resides at Rainbow Bridge or, that the soul goes to the Spirit World. But the fact is, that the soul does not die and that it does go somewhere, because Science and the Bible both confirm this fact. As a matter of fact, they both agree on many issues concerning the soul and the afterlife. In this book we will explore the afterlife both Scientifically and Biblically.

Science has proven that energy or spirits, never die; they only transfer somewhere else.

> Scientific Fact/Proof: *Scientists have proven that energy does not die or dissipate, it only transfers*

> *somewhere else. Law of Thermodynamics: Energy is neither created nor destroyed, it only transforms from one form to another. Our bodies collect energy and we lose energy.*
>
> (Source referenced: https://www.animalfacts.net/ Animals facts website. C. 2008 – 2019. Date accessed: March 2nd, 2019.)

Only recently have scientists discovered this fact, but they have not discovered how energy is created or where it comes from, but the Bible tells us how this energy is created and where it comes from.

The Bible also agrees with Science in the fact that energy does not die or dissipate as we can see in this next verse.

> Biblical Fact/Proof: *"I know that whatsoever God doeth, it shall be for ever…" (Ecclesiastes: 3:14)*

In the preceding verse, God says that He creates energy and that it lasts forever. The Bible, which was written thousands of years ago, tells us that energy does not die; long before man discovered this fact and it states that God created these energies with His breath, which creates a spirit in each creature; including animals. God creates all energies and spirits in Heaven and on earth.

The following verses tell us that God creates all of creation with His breath:

Biblical Fact/Proof: *"By the word of the LORD, were the heavens made; and all the host of them by the breath of his mouth." (Psalm 33:6)*

Biblical Fact/Proof: *"For by him were all things created, that are in heaven, and that are in the earth…" (Colossians:1:16)*

God sends out his spirit and creates all living creatures in Heaven and on the earth. Each living entity has the spirit of God.

Biblical Fact/Proof: *"Thou sendest forth thy spirit, they are created: and thou renewest the face of the earth." (Psalm: 104:30)*

We know that the soul or the spirit is energy. Both Science and the Bible inform us that the soul is a separate entity from the body.

Scientific Fact/Proof: *Your body is energy, your mind is energy, and your soul is energy. The difference is only of a different rhythm, and different wave lengths.*

(Source referenced OSHO website: c. 2019. Date accessed; March 3rd. https://www.osho.com/meditate/meditation-tool-kit/questions-about-meditation/what-is-the-relationship-between-consciousness-and-energy).

Science cannot explain where or how consciousness or energy comes from. The Bible tells us that energy is a spirit and that it comes from the spirit of God; because God is a spirit.

The Bible tells us that God preserves both man and beast. The next verse is more proof that our souls, and the souls of animals will live forever using the word "preservest".

> Biblical Fact/Proof: *"Thy righteousness is like the great mountains; thy judgments are a great deep: O LORD, thou preservest man and beast."* *(Psalm 36:6)*

The definition of the word preserve according to Webster's dictionary is: *"To keep alive or in existence. To keep safe from harm or injury; to protect or spare. To keep up or maintain."* *(Page 1046)*

God is telling us that the souls of all creatures will be keep in existence and live forever. God preserves our souls along with the souls of animals. Our souls do not die; they only transfer, and this includes animals, because animals have souls. Where does this energy go? The Bible gives us an explanation; but science cannot. The Bible tells us that the soul transfers to Heaven and into eternity.

The next verse describes what Heaven is like. It is like the Garden of Eden, and this verse tells us that animals are in Heaven and that there is only pure love, and that all creatures will live in harmony together.

> Bible Fact/Proof: *"The wolf also shall dwell with the lamb, and the leopard shall lie down with the kid; and the calf and the young lion and the fatling together; and a little child will lead them."* (Isaiah 11:6)

The Bible tells us that energy lasts forever thousands of years before scientists knew this fact. Animals and humans have souls and both science and the Bible also tell us that all souls last forever.

So now we know both Scientifically and Biblically, that our souls never die. Now, it is your choice to decide for yourself where these souls go. *Because we now know that they go somewhere!*

I believe that they go to Heaven, but that is my belief and I respect all beliefs. This book was not written to persuade or preach, but to present the facts both Scientifically and Biblically as they are, and to let you choose what you believe. We must look at both views both Scientific and Biblical, in order to know the truth.

There is an old saying that goes like this; *"If you close your mind, the only thing you will ever learn is what you already know."*

Chapter Two

LOSING A BELOVED PET

Losing a beloved pet can be devastating. I lost two pets in a year and a half. I lost Petie, a Boston Terrier and BJ, a Shih-Tzu; whom I rescued from abuse. First Petie went, then ten months later BJ passed. If that wasn't bad enough, soon after BJ passed, my cockatiel Co-Co Baby passed. Petie was over 15 years of age, BJ was almost 15 years of age, and Co-Co was a little over 20 years of age.

Our physical, mental, and spiritual health can be affected with the grief of losing a beloved animal. Grief is *caused* by our unconditional love for our beloved animal which upon death, temporarily separates our souls, which separates our spiritual bond with our animal. However, our love still remains, and this love will bond us once again in eternity.

We think of our pets as our children and most of us who own pets feel the same effects as when we lose a human who is dear to us. People who do not know this unconditional love for animals cannot understand how we feel, and they think we are crazy. We are not crazy. We have been given a special love that they do not have. We have been blessed with a supernatural or spiritual love, and it is a special gift.

Our pets are privy to our personal lives, such as our feelings, habits, moods, and our likes and our dislikes. We are closer to our animals than we are with most people, including some family members. Unlike people, they are with us on a constant basis. They don't grow up and leave home and they don't move out of town. They are with us through thick and thin, through all our happy times, and all our sad times. They are there when we need them, and we bond with them through our unconditional love. *We have a personal and unique relationship with our pets.*

Love is a real living spirit, or entity. We cannot grasp it or see it, but we know it is real because *we can feel it spiritually.* You may say, "Well Steven, I can see love when two people hug each other." No. You can see its effects, but you cannot see love "itself". You can *feel* love because it is a spirit. When people say they can *see* the love in the eyes of their pets, they are right. But this is "spiritual seeing" or feeling. The eyes are the windows to the soul and the next verse tells us that love is a spirit.

> Biblical Fact/Proof: *"For god has not given us the spirit of fear; but of power and of love, and of a sound mind." (2 Timothy 1:7)*

This scripture tells us that love is a spirit and all feelings and emotions are spirit driven. Even the bad emotions, which come from the Evil one.

In the next verse, the Bible describes unconditional love:

> Biblical Fact/Proof: *"Charity suffereth long, and is kind; charity envieth not; charity vaunteth not itself, is not puffed up, Doth not behave itself unseemly, seeketh not her own, is not easily provoked, thinketh no evil; Rejoiceth not in iniquity, but rejoiceth in the truth; Beareth all things, believeth all things, hopeth all things, endureth all things."*
> *(1 Corinthians 13: 4-7)*

The Bible is talking about love and using the word "charity". Love and charity are the same. The love or charity that God is describing is what we call, *"unconditional love, or agape love"*. This is the true meaning of unconditional love. God described unconditional love thousands of years ago in the Bible. This is the love that we animal lovers have, and therefore it is hard for us when we lose a beloved animal.

Science has only recently found out the beneficial effects of love.

> Scientific Fact/Proof: *Scientists, Physicians, and Psychiatrists have done studies on the effects of*

> *love and companionship with humans, as well as with animals. They reduce stress, give us better heart health, stronger relationships, better quality of sleep, and improved mental health.*
>
> Source referenced: Medical News Today website: Published on June 2, 2017. https://www.scientificstyleandformat.org/Tools/SSF-Citation-Quick-Guide.html. Date accessed: March 3rd, 2019.

Love can raise the level of dopamine in your body which stimulates pleasure. Love is a positive and healthy emotion and it raises the serotonin levels which creates well-being and a form of obsessiveness, or in other words; addiction. Yes, we are addicted to love! We are addicted to the love of our animals.

These hormones and chemicals that love produce are beneficial to our health by reducing stress. Scientists, Doctors, and Psychiatrists now claim that owning a pet reduces stress, makes a person happier, teaches loyalty, tolerance, unconditional love, responsibility, and many other positive traits. They have also found that animals have a positive and lasting effect on children who grow up around animals. Scientists also state that owning a pet, adds more years to a pet owner's life.

The Bible has already informed us of this fact and agrees with science. The next verse shows us how beneficial and important animals are and how they can help with stress, which can prolong our lives.

Biblical Fact/Proof: *"If a bird's nest chance to be before thee in the way in any tree, or on the ground, whether they be young ones, or eggs, and the dam sitting upon the young, or upon the eggs, thou shalt not take the dam with their young. But thou shalt in any wise let the dam go and take the young to thee; that it may be well with thee, and that thou mayest prolong thy days."* (Deuteronomy 22: 6-7)

It says, *"…and that thou mayest prolong thy days…"*. The Bible is telling us what Scientists and Psychiatrists have only discovered lately. Caring for animals not only prolongs our lives and promotes our emotional well-being, but animals also help take care of our environment. Without animals to balance our environment we would surely die. While in Heaven God told me that if He took all the humans of the earth, the animals would not only survive; they would thrive, but if He took all the animals off the earth, we would surely die. If we are truly honest, we must admit that we owe the animals our very existence because *we couldn't live without them.*

Chapter Three

SCIENCE AND THE BIBLE PROVE THAT ANIMALS HAVE SOULS

Many animals protect us, and they perform vital life-saving services such as; Police and Military dogs which save lives daily. Can you imagine being in a wartime situation and depending on an animal to save your life? I can only imagine the love and bonding between a policeman, or military person and his, or her dog.

Webster's definition of the word "animal" is as follows: *life; breath. (page 53);* which coincides with the Bible.

> Scientific Fact/Proof: *The word "animal" derives from the same root as "animate"' which means to move, or to make move, which comes from the Latin word, "animatus", and is the past participle of "animare" which means to give life to, which is based on the word, "anima" which basically*

means, "breath". It also means "soul" and any living thing that is composed of cells.

> (Source referenced: Merriam-Webster – Word Central website. (http://wordcentral.com/cgi-bin/student?animal). C. 2007. Referenced on March 3rd, 2019.

The Bible informs us that God sends forth His spirit, which comes from his "breath". He breathes life and a spirit into all living things, and He renews the earth. This simply means that God breathes His Spirit into all life, which includes animals.

All emotions and feelings come from the soul and we can clearly see this in our animals. We know they have feelings, so therefore we know they have souls. We know that they respond to the world and environment such as; they fear danger, they relax when things are calm, they worry when we are gone from home, and many other feelings just like humans.

Let's find out the definition of two important words; *Soul and Spirit*.

Webster's defines the word "soul" as:

> **1.** *"the principal of life, feeling, thought, and actions in humans, regarded as a distinct entity separate from the body.* **2.** *The spiritual part of humans regarded in its moral aspect, or as believed to survive death and be subject to happiness or misery in a life to come." (page 1253)*

This definition states that the soul is the *"principal of life"* and is a distinct entity from the body. We know that animals have souls and spirits, because they like us, have life, feelings, thoughts, and actions. Webster also states that the soul survives death and although it points out humans, we know that animals have the same traits of feelings, thoughts, and actions. Animals do have souls, or they would not be alive.

Now let's find out what "spirit" means. Webster's dictionary says;

> *1. "the animating principle of life, **esp. of humans**; vital essence. 2. The incorporeal part of humans, or an aspect of this, as the mind or soul. 3. Conscious, incorporeal being, as opposed to matter. 4. A supernatural, incorporeal being, esp. one having a particular character: evil spirits." (page 1265)*

The spirit is the animating principle of *life* and this definition says especially of humans. The word "especially" means that Webster is including animals but is concerned mainly with humans. Let's find out what the word especially means. Especially is defined by Webster's dictionary as: *"to an exceptional degree; particularly; in particular." (page 450)*

What Webster's definition is saying is; that everything living has a soul, but Webster is pointing out that he and most people, are more concerned about humans in particular, and because of this "particular" concern of only humans, people who read the Bible have missed almost eighty verses that prove animals have souls and do go to Heaven.

The definition also says, *"vital essence"*. The word "essence" means; *"a spiritual or immaterial entity"*. (page 451)

The word *incorporeal* is used and so is the word *supernatural*. Notice also that it says *evil* spirits too. The word "life" is important in this definition too because animals have life. They are alive. If a creature is alive, then it has a soul and it also has a spirit. Animals have souls and we bond to these souls with the spirit that is known as "love" and we now know that the soul does not die. The spirit is the energy, or fuel that drives the soul. The soul is you; your personality; what makes you…you, and the soul is what gives your pet his, or her personality. We know that animals have souls too because they have their own personalities. We also know from experience that when a human or an animal passes, something goes missing from the body; which of course is the soul.

I will use the word "soul" mostly in this book rather than spirit, but they are basically the same. One is energy (the spirit) and one (the soul) is what we do with this energy.

Scientists and the Bible both agree that there is a separate entity (corporeal or supernatural) that is called a soul, and that it never dies. They both agree that it is necessary to have a soul to be alive. So therefore, we know that everything that lives has a soul.

The scripture below states that the soul does not die, but lives eternally:

> Biblical Fact/Proof: *Jesus looked up to Heaven and prayed to God saying, "Father, the hour is come, glorify thy Son, that thy Son also may glorify thee: As thou hast given him power over all flesh, that he should give eternal life to as many as thou hast given him." (John 17: 1-2)*

What this scripture is telling us is, that God has given Jesus the power to give eternal life to every living soul, which includes animals. And we know this because it says, "all flesh". Now we know that the souls of our pets are in Heaven waiting for our souls to join and bond with them in eternity, by the spirit called love; and Heaven is love.

Chapter Four

SCIENCE AND THE BIBLE PROVE THAT ANIMALS ARE CAPABLE OF THINKING AND REASONING

Animals have many feelings and traits that we humans have. We have all seen videos or have personally observed how animals protect and take care of other animals, (some not their own kind) and humans too. Animals are able to plan ahead and accomplish tasks. They have social connections, thought processes, and emotions. How many times have we seen dogs when they are happy, scared, mad, protective, embarrassed, or slink under the bed, or under a table from guilt. And don't forget something very important; animals also like to play just like us! They enjoy pleasure and recreational activities too. In order to play, one must have cognitive abilities, which we know is an action of the soul, and the action of playing is a necessary element of the soul. If there is any action that proves that animals have souls, it is the ability to play. Playing involves thinking, feeling, reasoning, enjoyment/

happiness, communicating, a sense of humor, planning ahead, and play is an act of friendship and love.

> Scientific Proof/ Fact: *Scientists agree that playing is related to humor. Humor and play show the ability to reason, feel, think, and to plan ahead, and animals display these qualities. These attributes must exist, in order to be able to play. Many animals can be taught tricks too, both simple and complex tricks. This shows without a doubt, that animals can think and reason.*
>
> (Source referenced: All You Need is Biology website: https://allyouneedisbiology.wordpress.com/2016/04/09/play-in-animals/. C. 2016. Date accessed: March 3rd, 2019).

> Scientific Fact/Proof: *Scientists have studied animals at play and have concluded that they are just like us. The reason for play is to develop social skills, form social bonds, adjust to their environment, and to relieve any fear or anxieties they may have. Almost all animals engage in play with each other, other animals, and humans.*
>
> (Source referenced: All You Need is Biology website: https://allyouneedisbiology.wordpress.com/2016/04/09/play-in-animals/. C. 2016. Date accessed: March 3rd, 2019).

Scientific Fact/Proof: *Playing is linked to morality, intelligence, thinking, reasoning, and spirituality. Animals display morals when playing.*

(Source referenced: All You Need is Biology website: https://allyouneedisbiology.wordpress.com/2016/04/09/play-in-animals/. C. 2016. Date accessed: March 3rd, 2019).

A good example is: A dog knows just how hard to bite without harming the person or animal who is playing with him and of course, love is also involved in the act of playing

The Bible states that God plays with His animals. In this next verse God asks Job if he can play with the Leviathan:

"Wilt thou play with him as with a bird?" (Job 41: 2-5)

God is asking Job if he can play with this huge beast and of course Job cannot, but God says that He does. God says that He plays with all His animals no matter how big, or how small.

In order to love, care, and play with another being, means that a creature or being, must be able to think and reason and all pet owners know this to be a fact.

How many times when we feel sad that our animals are sad with us? They know when something is wrong with us and they show empathy towards our feelings. This alone proves they have emotions, and that they can think and reason. When my daughter-in-law was pregnant, my dog Petie knew it and he would lie beside her and protect her.

BJ was upset when Petie passed and he went in the bedroom and hid. He was scared and grieving too. BJ and I got even closer after Peite's death. BJ knew I was sad, and he too was grieving along with me. His spirit sensed my feelings of sadness and this increased the bond that we had.

I rescued BJ from abuse, and he had PTSD (Post Traumatic Syndrome Disorder). This is just a fancy word for trauma and is mostly associated with war veterans, but it is caused by any type of trauma such as abuse, a bad car wreck, or any other traumatic incident or injury. In order to have PTSD you *must have a reasoning, cognitive ability*; or in other words, a soul. Every animal lover has seen at least one abused animal and how they developed mental and emotional issues from this abuse.

We are not very far from being animals ourselves because we have so many shared characteristics. Like us, animals exhibit ambitions for a higher status, they compete for food, sex, and many other of the same traits that we exhibit. They strive to stay alive and to seek and build shelter and both humans and animals raise and care for their young.

> Scientific Fact/Proof: *Many Scientists are beginning to discover through recent studies and research, that we share many of the same traits with the animals*

than was previously thought because the subject was ignored.

(Source referenced: National Geographic website: https://news.nationalgeographic.com/2015/07/150714-animal-dog-thinking-feelings-brain-science/. C. 2019. Date referenced: March 4th, 2019.)

So, if a creature is thinking, then they are conscious and if they are conscious, they have a soul. People and animals obviously do share many of the same traits. In the verse below King Solomon states:

Biblical Fact/Proof: *"I said in mine heart concerning the estate of the sons of men, that God might manifest them, and that they might see that they themselves are beasts." (Ecclesiastes: 3: 18)*

King Solomon is considered to be the wisest man in the history of the world. King Solomon is praying that God would make men aware that they too are animals, and that men are no better than animals. He is also telling us that we are no different than the animals. I have seen some animals act like people, and I have seen some people act like animals. The only difference between humans and animals is that we have a cerebral cortex and a brain stem, and animals have only a brain stem, and animals have only a brain stem. But the brain stem has energy, intellect, feelings, emotions, and a soul.

Chapter Five

SCIENCE AND THE BIBLE PROVE THAT ANIMALS HAVE FEELINGS

Are animals capable of love, loyalty, guilt, embarrassment, shame, and happiness? Can animals teach us things, such as moral and ethical values? The answer is yes to all the above. All those who own pets know this without question because we see these emotional traits and actions every day in our beloved animals.

Animals can and do teach us many things. They teach us morals, values, unconditional love, compassion, loyalty, and much more. *These are all qualities of the soul.* Most animals have emotions and feelings such as sadness, anger, happiness, shame, guilt, and each animal is endowed with a different and unique personality, which shows that they too have souls.

> Biblical Fact/Proof: *"Who teacheth us more than the beasts of the earth, and maketh us wiser than the fowls of heaven?" (Job: 35: 11)*

In this verse, God is telling Job (and us) that we can and do learn from His animals. God is saying, that animals are second only to Him in teaching us about morals, values, unconditional love, and many other attributes. The Bible tells us that we can be wiser than the birds that are in Heaven. In my vision, God told me to be more like a dog because I had a hard time with forgiveness.

Animals are said to have ten human attributes which are; culture, emotions, language, humor, memory, self-awareness, intelligence, farming, building, the ability to play, and the ability to use tools.

> Scientific Fact/Proof: *Research has shown that animals have feelings and emotions. They teach us about unconditional love and empathy. They like to cuddle. They need companionship, and they take care of their young as we do. They help each other, they can communicate with each other and can even communicate with humans. They can be diplomatic, and they respect their elders. They show us how to love unconditionally and they teach us forgiveness.*
>
> (Source referenced: Life Wellness website by Carolyn Gregoire. https://www.huffpost.com/entry/proof-that-animals-are-wa_n_4255262?guccounter=1. Updated Dec. 7, 2017. Referenced on March 4th, 2019.

Chapter Six

VISIONS OF HEAVEN AND NEAR DEATH EXPERIENCES

Many people have had NDE's. (Near Death Experiences). This phenomenon happens when a person dies for a short period of time and comes back to life, either on their own, or resuscitated by a doctor. These people claim that they went to Heaven in the short time that they were clinically dead. They claim to have seen loved ones who have passed, and they also state that they have seen animals; be it their own animals, or just animals in Heaven. (We will explore true NDE experiences in chapter Ten.)

These people have died during a surgical procedure, having been involved in a car wreck, or some other type of traumatic incident where they have died for a short period of time, but came back to life. They claim to have the feeling of floating above their bodies from the area of the ceiling. They observe not only their bodies, but also all the actions of those that are present in the room such as, doctors or family members. They describe traveling through a tunnel that leads to a bright light. Many have stated that they were taken straight to Heaven and have interacted with their pets and their relatives. Some people claim they are told that it isn't their time yet and that they must return. Others claim that they are given the choice to stay or return to their earthly bodies.

There are also people that have open trance visions, or prophetic dreams. Many of the patriarchs of the Bible and prophets of modern times have had open trance visions. This is where a person has a vision and is taken to Heaven through intense prayer while alive. I have had several open trance visions and in one of my visions I was taken to Heaven to see my dog BJ and all my other dogs that I have owned in my lifetime. I believe many of these claims are true because I have experienced the same things that they have described. These people can tell you things about their experience that they could not have possibly known before. I too, knew things after my vision that I couldn't have possibly ever known before.

Many times, these people have given testimonies that cannot be disputed. For instance, they can describe the actions of people and the items in the room that they could not have possibly known about because they were clinically dead. One boy who had an NDE claimed he met a relative that he never knew about or was ever told about, and he described the relative in detail. When his parents showed him a picture of this relative in a photo book of many other people, the boy picked out the correct picture. This is more than coincidence.

> Scientific Fact/Proof: *NDE's are very common place. Scientists, Psychologists, and Physicians are divided on the validity of these phenomenal experiences. Some believe they are real, and others claim that it can be explained neurologically.*
>
> (Source referenced: The Atlantic website. https://www.theatlantic.com/magazine/archive/2015/04/the-science-of-near-death-experiences/386231/. C. April 2016. Date referenced: March 4th, 2019).

Scientists and Psychologists who say that these experiences are from the mind have never proven it one way or the other. They are unable to explain how people who have died and have information that they could not have possibly known otherwise while they were clinically dead. Many skeptics who have had NDE's have converted to Christianity after having an NDE experience.

I have a degree in psychology, and I have been a substance abuse and family counselor. I have always believed in the Scientific method and have always questioned my visions, trying to disprove them because I didn't want to be crazy, but the more I tried to disprove them, the more I proved them to be true.

Scientists and Psychiatrists can neither prove, nor disprove whether these NDE experiences are divine or only a psychological experience of the unknowable mind. They can only present their "theories" which is only their opinion. They have been completely unable to explain how these people can describe things that happened while they were dead. Or in cases where some people who had maladies or terminal illnesses have been completely cured after their experience. Their only defense is; the mind is unfathomable. That is not proof in any way, it is only an opinion.

Many of the patriarchs of the Bible had open trance visions, one such person that had an open trance vision was the Apostle Peter. His vision included many types of animals that *came from Heaven and went back to Heaven.*

> Biblical Fact/Proof: "...heaven opened, and a certain vessel descended unto him, as it had been a great sheet knit at the four corners and let down to earth: Wherein there were all manner of four-footed beasts of the earth, and wild beasts, and creeping things, and fowls of the earth...this was done thrice ; and the vessel was received up again into heaven" (Acts 10: 11-16)

In this verse, we can clearly see that God is telling us in precise words that *animals are in Heaven.* As you can see, they came from Heaven and went back to Heaven.

The following verse is another proof that our animals will be in Heaven when they pass.

> Biblical Fact/Proof: *"And all flesh shall see the salvation of God." (Luke 3: 6)*

The Bible tells us in this verse that there *is* a Heaven; for salvation is Heaven and it states *all flesh*, which includes animals. Animals will be in Heaven too, along with humans. Most Scientists believe in an afterlife, another dimension, an alternative universe, or Heaven where the soul resides after death.

The Bible also tells us that God loves His animals as much as He loves humans. Does God love His animals enough to preserve them and take them to Heaven? Here is the proof:

> Biblical Fact/Proof: *"Consider the ravens; for they neither sow nor reap; which neither have storehouse nor barn; and God feedeth them: how much more are ye better than the fowls?" (Luke 12:24)*

The word "better" as defined in Webster's dictionary means: *"Morally superior. Knowing the distinction between right and wrong." (page 128)*

This definition means that we humans know right from wrong; animals do not. The word *"superior"* only means higher in rank.

Just as the Bible tells us that the Jewish people have a higher rank than Gentiles; but God loves us all the same, but in a different way. God has a different love for each soul. I love my sons the same, but I have a different love for each son, and a different love for my wife.

The Bible tells us that we are only morally superior (better) than animals. *Nowhere in the Bible does God say that He loves us more than the animals.* God says that we are only morally superior than the animals because we know right from wrong and we are supposed to have values and morals; animals have instinct.

Animals are sinless and innocent, but we are not. God loves all His creatures and each creature receives a different love. God's love for you is different than His love for me *because each soul is different.*

The Bible tells us that God so loved the world that He gave His only son. If you notice it says, *"God so loved the world"* and this includes animals.

> Biblical Fact/Proof: *"For God so loved the world, that he gave his only begotten son…" (John 3: 16)*

Webster's definition of the word, *"world"* is: *"The earth with its inhabitants, affairs; Everything that exists in the earth."* *(page 1507)*

As you can see, Jesus came to save not only us, but the animals too from this corrupted world. This whole world is corrupted and everything in it.

A side note: The Bible tells us that there is good news and there is bad news. It tells us that animals are sinless and that they go to heaven automatically. However, the Bible states that if you are not saved and you don't believe in Jesus, you will not be going to Heaven to be with your animal. The Bible tells us that there is only one way to heaven for humans, and that is through the belief in Jesus. You can choose to believe, or not to believe the Bible. This is your right to believe as you wish.

Chapter Seven

WHY DO I GRIEVE?

When our beloved pet passes, we think we will never get over it, but we will; and we do. This is a natural feeling and all animal lovers experience this feeling of despair. We feel many emotions at one time, and they overwhelm us. Feelings of sadness, loneliness, anger, guilt, loss, and even lethargy. We wonder if the pain will ever subside or go away and we feel as though a part of us has been taken too. This is because our soul and our pet's soul has been separated. When BJ died, I felt as though I had died too because the bonding of our souls had been separated. When our soul bonds with an animal (or human) soul, our soul merges with that soul and we in a sense, become one with that animal. When your animal passes, it splits the soul bond, and a part of you is gone. The soul of your animal that you were merged with, is gone. But as stated, your soul will be bonded with your animal into eternity once again and it will be a much stronger bond. This is important for you to understand in order to heal.

We become lethargic to the point that we almost give up on life. We know when we adopt an animal that they do not live very long, however we adopt anyway due to our unconditional love. We tell ourselves that it will be just fine, and our new pet will live a long time. Our love pushes the thought of death out of our minds and we adopt. We couldn't very well leave the animal to fend for itself or take the chance that no one will adopt it, or that it may be put down. Our unconditional love allows us to push any bad thoughts to the side and we adopt.

When you lose a pet, it is important to know that the time you had with your animal was a gift. You and your pet's soul were bound by your unconditional love and you must always remember that *the time you had with your beloved animal was well worth the pain of losing them.*

One of the main reasons we have such a hard time after the loss of a pet is due to the fact, that it is a personal process that one usually goes through *on their own* because many people do not understand the feelings and the love we had for our beloved animals. When a human being passes, it is socially acceptable and customary to feel empathy for the one who has lost a relative or a friend. When our beloved animal passes, it is not socially acceptable nor customary to give sympathy. Many people say, *"It's just an animal"* but to us, it is more than just an animal. We think of our pet as a family member and the pain is equal to losing a beloved relative, but sadly, many people don't think that way.

They do not know or understand the unconditional love that we have for our animals and they are incapable or, unwilling to bond with the soul of an animal like we can. We are special and we have a special love, and this unconditional love is a gift.

We think of our pets as our children. We feed them, we walk them, we care for their health, we sleep with them, we talk to them, and give we them our all, including our private whims and feelings. They provide us with emotional support, unconditional love, loyalty, forgiveness, and constant companionship when humans fail to give us these things. We share things with our animals that we would never share with another human being. I trust my animals more than I do most people.

I had a hound dog named Duke and he was my brother and my best friend. I grew up in an alcoholic home and he was my whole world. I really don't think I would be alive today had it not been for his love and constant companionship. When he passed it rocked my world, but I knew I had to go on. *For me, the time I had with my animals was well worth the pain of losing them.*

Our unconditional love and our special ability to bond with the soul of an animal leaves us vulnerable to grief when we lose our beloved pet. But the good news is; we will be reunited with them upon our death in eternity. In my vision, God told me that he missed BJ too and that it was time for him to *come home*. God told me that all the animals that I ever had would be waiting for me in Heaven. He also reminded me that I did not create BJ, nor did I have any claim to him, and that BJ was a gift. God said that he was proud of me for taking care of *His* animals. When we pass, we will be reunited with our animals in eternity, and the word eternity basically means, without end.

Chapter Eight

AM I CRAZY FOR GRIEVING OVER MY ANIMAL?

No! You are not crazy, you were blessed with a special love that many do not have; or know. Don't let guilt command or run your feelings. Don't let sadness or guilt distort and suppress your love of animals and keep you from adopting another animal.

There will be some people who will make fun of you, try to bully you, and make you feel guilty. Especially if you must put your pet down, or if it escapes from the house and gets lost or killed. Pay no attention to these people. Talk to someone who knows and understands.

Pet loss is a real mental, physical, and spiritual condition. When we lose a pet, we have many emotions that overwhelm us because it is just as real, and no different than losing a close friend, or family member. We have a loss of appetite, we cry, we are in shock, we are angry, we suffer with insomnia, guilt, sadness, depression and we isolate ourselves. Some people may lose the zest for life and even contemplate suicide. Don't do that or you will never see your pet again. Guilt is probably the most dominant feeling. As stated, you have nothing to feel guilty about. Don't focus on the times you had to scold your pet, or anything negative. Focus on all the good memories. Remember, you gave your animal a wonderful life and more than enough love. Your animal is waiting for you in Heaven, but you must finish your journey too and just as important remember that *you saved your last pet's life* by giving it a loving and safe home. You may not realize it but when you adopted your pet and gave it love and a home, you were a hero. Give yourself credit for saving your last animal's life and giving it a loving and safe home.

Science and phycologists have found that pet loss is an emotional experience and causes depression:

> Scientific Fact/Proof: *You will have a loss of interest in your usual activities, a loss of pleasurable things you normally do. You will be somewhat confused, and your cognitive process will be disoriented. You will suffer from a lack of identity and you will begin to wonder what life is about. You will seem to lack energy and you will feel tired. These are all signs of depression which is normal; the same as if you had lost a family member.*

(Source referenced: I am not ashamed; Billy Graham Association website. https://psychcentral.com/lib/grieving-the-loss-of-a-pet/ by Julie Axelrod. Last update: 8 Oct., 2018. Referenced on March 4th, 2019.

I can't stress it enough to avoid any feelings of guilt. It isn't your fault that your beloved animal has passed because you gave your beloved animal all the love you could. If you must euthanize your animal, do not feel guilty. It is far better to let them go if they are suffering. Let them go on to Heaven but stay with them until they pass; this is very important. Your face should be the last thing they see.

Know that you will be reunited with them in eternity where nothing grows old and nothing dies. If you are a Christian, you may wonder why you mourn the loss of a pet more than you do some humans. This is because when we read the Bible we have been conditioned to focus on the human aspect of the Bible. We know humans go to Heaven, but we still wonder if animals do, and so that is a big part of the mourning process; not knowing and wondering if your animal is in Heaven or not. The Bible contains almost eighty scriptures that prove animals do go to Heaven, but most people tend to overlook these proofs because they are focused on the "human" aspect of the Bible. Read my first and second books for all the proof. They each contain over forty scriptural proofs each. These books were written for healing too.

In the following verse the Bible tells us that God gathers all souls to himself. He saves all souls and we know animals have souls.

> Biblical Fact/Proof: *"That in the dispensation of the fullness of times he might gather together in one all things in Christ, both which are in heaven, and which are on earth; even in him."* (Ephesians 1:10).

The Bible tells us that Jesus will take all souls to Heaven because the scripture reads, *"he gathers all things"*. This includes our precious animals too. Have faith and be joyful that your animal is in Heaven waiting for your arrival. You will be with your beloved animals for eternity.

And just as importantly; adopt again and share your unconditional love with another animal. There are many animals out there waiting for someone to love them. Satan doesn't want you to adopt because he hates love, and everything that God has created, including us.

In summary, pet loss is a real and normal emotional reaction. Focus only on the good memories. Do not let guilt or any other negative thoughts and feelings depress you. Have a memorial service for your pet and talk only with those who have our special gift of love. Know that your beloved animals are waiting for you to join them in eternity and that they are in a wonderful place where there is no pain, sorrow, hunger, thirst, abuse, or death; only love. And lastly, please adopt again. *Don't waste your love by not loving!*

Chapter Nine

HOW DO I RECOVER FROM MY LOSS?

When my dog BJ passed, I was crushed. I had feelings of loneliness, guilt, anger, and depression. I was lethargic, and I felt physically ill and I didn't care about life and I felt as though there was nothing to live for. I cried for a long time and I was scared to go to work the first week for fear of crying in front of other people. I know the pain of pet loss.

I always believed in my heart that animals went to Heaven, but when BJ passed, I had to know. I wanted absolute proof, and nothing else would suffice. I asked people if they thought that animals went to Heaven and they all said, *"No"*, *"Gee I don't know"*, *"Maybe"*, *"Yes, I think so"*, and *"Who knows?"* I even asked some ministers and I got the same various answers. Finally, out of desperation, I took it to God for an answer and I was given a divine vision (I wrote of this experience in my first book).

Do not try to replace your new animal with the exact kind you just lost, thinking it will be the exact same. If you lost a Collie, don't think that if you get another Collie, they will be the same. Each animal like humans, have different souls and personalities. I made that mistake after BJ passed and I went on the internet searching various animal shelter sites looking for a dog that looked and acted just like BJ, hoping that he would be the same as BJ in every way. Grief will make us do silly things because grief affects our thinking and reasoning. I'm not saying not to get a dog of the same breed as you had, I'm saying don't expect the new dog to be the same as the one that has recently passed. Each animal has a different soul, and therefore a different personality.

You can never replace a beloved animal however you can learn to love the soul of a different animal. Loving a new animal *is more medicinal than you can imagine*. The Bible says that love cures all things. The different and special soul of another animal is a different experience with a new and different love. There are thousands of animals that need adopting and just think, there will be another animal that will be there to meet you in Heaven.

Recovering from pet loss may take time but there are steps to shorten the process and lessen the pain. Knowing that BJ was in Heaven waiting for me, took a lot of pain away and brought me joy. Of course, we will never get over it completely and we will certainly miss our pet, but these steps and the information in this book can help you to accept the loss and move on to love again. Just knowing for certain that your beloved pet is in Heaven waiting for you can bring you hope and joy as it did me.

Have a memorial service for you beloved pet and most importantly, take care of yourself and keep busy. Look for things to be grateful for and cherish the good memories you had with your pet. If there is another pet in the house, turn your attention to them, because believe it or not, they are most likely suffering the loss too and they will also sense your feelings of sadness. If children are involved, allow them to express their grief and feelings too. Make it a family affair.

Keep in mind that our love bonds us to that animal and this love will reunite you and your beloved animal when you pass and enter eternity. Your spirits have been temporarily severed until you meet them again in eternity. Our souls are bonded when they are here, but not fully. When we meet them in the afterlife, our souls will not only bond with theirs, but we will be fully bonded forever in the spiritual realm. This realm is pure spirit and love.

For those who believe in God and in Heaven, you will be amazed at the spirit realm. I have been there, and it is a place that is impossible to describe, and I only saw a small portion of it.

Visions and NDE's are supernatural. The word supernatural originally began with God. Satan is supernatural too, but he is evil. Supernatural simply means, "not of this earth", or "another dimension" or, "the spirit world", or "Heaven". If you believe in Heaven and hell then you should know these facts: Satan's name while in Heaven was Lucifer, which means, "bringer of light." God changed Lucifer's name to Satan (when he fell from grace) which means, "adversary". It is important to know this because you must remember that Satan is our adversary. He will try anything to make you feel guilty, sad, angry, depressed, and despondent; and any other bad feelings and emotions that he can stir up in you after the loss of your pet. He will use the death of your pet to make you miserable and to doubt God's goodness. Satan is the one who brought death to the world.

My point being; do not feel guilty about the loss of your pet. Your beloved pet is in a place that you could never imagine with the greatest owner there is. I remember when BJ passed, I felt all kinds of guilt. Did the medicine that the vet gave me shorten his life? What if there were some chemicals in it that killed him? Why didn't I spend more time with him? Could I have fed him better? Maybe the food had chemicals in it that killed him? Was there something I could have done different? No! These are the thoughts that Satan *wants* you to think. He loves it when we beat ourselves up and he laughs at us when we do this because he wants us to be miserable or dead. I remember BJ's last few days were torture for me and I called the Vet's office to inquire how much it would cost to put him down. I was an emotional wreck knowing that BJ was suffering terribly. It was killing me to watch him suffer and I felt totally helpless. BJ passed a few minutes after the phone call and I was glad and devastated at the same time.

If you must put your animal down, don't feel guilty about it. Would you rather that they suffer? Why, that's no different than torture or abuse. If you must put them down no matter how much it hurts, don't leave them in a strange office alone. If you must put your beloved animal down, stay with them until they pass. It will ease their passing to know that their beloved is with them. As soon as they pass, God will be there to collect their soul and take them to Heaven in the blink of an eye. The following verse proves this fact.

> Biblical Fact/Proof: *"Are not two sparrows sold for a farthing? And one of them shall not fall on the ground without your Father." (Matthew 10: 29)*

In this verse, the Bible tells us that God is there to take the souls of these birds to Heaven upon the instant of death, and this includes all animals and people. And if the two sparrows in the above verse didn't have souls, why would God even fool with the dead bodies of these birds? And we know they are dead because it says, *"...shall not fall on the ground."* This tells us that the birds are dead, or they would be flying in the air not falling on the ground.

A farthing was worth about two cents. In the above verse, God is saying that men might not think much of animals; but He does. They are His because He created them. You must remember that

God created the animals; we didn't. We have no claim on them, only the Creator does.

And in the last verse, it states that these birds are not *forgotten* by God. Webster's definition of forgotten is: *"To cease to remember. To omit or neglect. To leave behind." (Page 515)*

This verse plainly states that God does not cease to remember, neglect, or leave behind the souls of animals. In this verse He is simply using birds to make His point because the Jewish people thought the sparrow was the lowest and cheapest animal at that time in Jewish History. But to God, no animal is cheap or lowly. *God is saying He loves all animals equally and that He takes their souls to Heaven*. If He didn't take them to Heaven, then the verse would read; "and all of them are forgotten."

Many people ask, *"Why did God take my animal from me?"* God told me in my vision that He missed BJ too. He told me *it was time for BJ to come back home to Him and that his mission was complete*. God loves and misses His animals the same as we do and we must remember, that all things die.

People ask, why does God allow animals to be abused. Wrong! Satan is the one who pushes people into doing this evil. People do this because God gives us all free will and God allows people to do what they want; be it good actions, or bad actions. God is not a dictator. Technically, we brought sin (Satan) into this world. Stop blaming God and blame the ones who are truly responsible; people and Satan. Satan does not want you to adopt and love another animal because he hates God and he knows that God loves us and everything that He created. Satan wants to destroy all that God has made because he hates God and us, and if Satan can get people to do his work for him, he will.

In summary, have faith that you will see your pet again. Know that your love will reunite you with your animal and that this life is very short. God has his reasons that we cannot understand; but trust Him no matter what. And lastly, do not feel any guilt at your loss, for it is Satan telling you this garbage to make you depressed, unhappy, and to make you hate and lose your faith in God. The Bible tells us in many places that Satan is the Great Deceiver. He is the master liar and he has had eons to hone his skills. Satan will make you feel guilty and depressed if you let him. Know that your animal is in a wonderful place, just waiting for your arrival in Heaven and eternity. And just as importantly, know that God is proud of you for taking care of His animal.

Adopt another animal. This helps more than you know. At first you will think two things; I just can't adopt right now, I am still grieving and when I do adopt, I want to find one exactly like the animal I just lost. One of the most common reasons not to adopt again is that we feel as though we would dishonor the memory of our deceased pet. We feel as though we are cheating on and betraying our animal. No! Your last pet would be honored that you have helped another animal.

About a month after BJ passed, I prayed to God and asked if I should adopt another dog and he showed me the dog that was for me. When I first saw Jasper, he wasn't what I expected at all. He wasn't a Shih-Tzu, but God in His infinite mercy gave me a dog that looked like both Petie and BJ and I love Jasper dearly.

It is alright to give it a little time, but don't wait too long. You will know when you are ready. I waited about a month. Your previous pet will be honored and happy that you adopted and saved another animal. Do not feel guilty for adopting, thinking your previous pet will be mad or jealous. Your pet is in Heaven and is in a much, much, better place.

Know that your animal is living a life of the greatest magnitude in Heaven; a place that you cannot possibly imagine. Think of only the good memories and shun any guilt or remorse. These are evil thoughts and not good for your health. Your animal would not like you killing yourself over his or her death. When I saw BJ in Heaven, he told me not worry or grieve anymore; he was finally home, and he had a young, beautiful, and vibrant body. His body glowed and I knew it was from God. When I saw my dogs in Heaven, *I felt inferior* to them because I knew that they had the knowledge of all the secrets of the universe. I could see it in their eyes, and I knew they were in their new eternal bodies and that they had the knowledge of the LORD; which is love.

Here is a verse that describes what I saw in their eyes:

Biblical Fact/Proof: *"They shall not hurt nor destroy in all my holy mountain; for the earth shall be full of the knowledge of the LORD, as the waters cover the seas." (Isaiah 11:6-9)*

This is what I saw in BJ's eyes. The knowledge of God! And God's knowledge is *love and wisdom*.

Grieving is a personal experience because not everyone knows how we feel. Reaching out to other people who are grieving the loss of a pet and understand how we feel is a great healing tool. There are plenty of internet sites for pet loss. I have one myself. Bury your animal and include a funeral and a headstone. I put a picture of BJ by my chair where I sit and one by my bed and if you have another pet in the house, give them solace for they are grieving too. Join a pet support group and don't be afraid to seek professional help.

Chapter Ten

TRUE STORIES OF ANIMALS THAT SAVED PEOPLE

Now let's examine how animals have helped people which gives us more proof that animals have souls. These true stories prove that animals can reason, think, and that they do have feelings and souls. These stories also show that animals have a cognitive process.

> *Story 1:* A Vietnamese pet pig named Lulu, noticed her owner fall to the floor and immediately went out in the street and laid down blocking traffic, regardless of her own life. Finally, someone stopped and followed Lulu to the house where they saw the woman lying on the floor and called for assistance, which saved the woman's life.
>
> (Source accessed: website: Animal Wised, by Josie F. Turner: https://www.animalwised.com/

top-10-unbelievable-animals-that-saved-people-s-lives-2475.html. Published 2019. Date referenced: March 4th, 2019).

How could a pig do this? Lulu had to be able to reason in order to know that its owner needed help. Lulu had to have a thinking and reasoning process that told her what needed to be done. It also shows that Lulu knew what love was.

Story 2: Jambo the gorilla saved a young boy's life at a zoo. When the child fell into the gorilla cage, Jambo came to his aid and took the young child in his arms and stroked the child's back to calm the boy down. Jambo then protected the child from the other gorillas until the zoo keepers could get the child.

(Source accessed: website: Animal Wised, by Josie F. Turner: https://www.animalwised.com/top-10-unbelievable-animals-that-saved-people-s-lives-2475.html. Published 2019. Date referenced: March 4th, 2019).

This shows a spirit of concern and the emotion of care. Jambo acted like a human by caring for another creature's life.

Story 3: A dog named Toby performed the Heimlich maneuver on his owner. Some people don't even know how to do this, and Toby never had a class on how to perform this maneuver. His owner was choking to death on a piece of apple and fell to the floor. Toby immediately jumped on her chest and dislodged the obstruction from the owner's throat, saving her life. This is a case where an animal used extreme reasoning. Toby knew that his owner was choking on something and acted accordingly, knowing exactly what needed to be done.

> (Source accessed: website: Animal Wised, by Josie F. Turner: https://www.animalwised.com/top-10-unbelievable-animals-that-saved-people-s-lives-2475.html. Published 2019. Date referenced: March 4th, 2019).

Story 4: In Africa, a young girl was kidnapped and left for dead in the jungle because she refused to marry a man that had been chosen for her. The police formed a search party to look for the missing girl. When they finally found her, there were three male lions guarding her. When the searchers approached the lions, they left and went into the jungle as if their jobs were done. This shows an emotion of caring and that the lions were communicating with each other in order to protect the young girl.

> (Source accessed: website: Animal Wised, by Josie F. Turner: https://www.animalwised.com/top-10-unbelievable-animals-that-saved-people-s-lives-2475.html. Published 2019. Date referenced: March 4th, 2019).

Story 5: In another amazing story, a goat named Mandy saved her owner's life. The man had fallen off his horse and had broken his hip. He was too far out to call for help and was on his own for five days. Mandy laid down and kept him warm and even allowed the man to drink her milk which nourished him and kept him alive until someone found him. Certainly, without a doubt, animals cannot act this way showing care and love, unless they are able to feel, think, and care for something other than themselves and we know that these are the actions of the soul.

> (Source accessed: website: Animal Wised, by Josie F. Turner: https://www.animalwised.com/top-10-unbelievable-animals-that-saved-people-s-lives-2475.html. Published 2019. Date referenced: March 4th, 2019).

Story 6: A dog named Kabang, deliberately pushed a woman and a little girl out of the way of an oncoming car, saving them from death or injury. Only a creature with a soul could do this. Kabang suffered minor wounds and later recovered.

> (Source accessed: website: Animal Wised, by Josie F. Turner: https://www.animalwised.com/top-10-unbelievable-animals-that-saved-people-s-lives-2475.html. Published 2019. Date referenced: March 4th, 2019).

I know some people that would not put themselves in harm's way to help another human. This dog was incredible. Kabang showed concern and the willingness to save another creature's life. Kabang knew that cars were dangerous, and his actions showed that he had an unconditional love, by putting his own life in jeopardy.

> *Story 7:* A German Shepherd in Australia named Dasher stayed with his young owner for fourteen hours protecting him from harm. A two-year old child named Dante walked out of the house and no one noticed but Dasher, the family dog. Dasher followed the little boy and they eventually got lost in the forest. They endured a bad storm before they were found.
>
> (Source accessed: website: Animal Wised, by Josie F. Turner: https://www.animalwised.com/top-10-unbelievable-animals-that-saved-people-s-lives-2475.html. Published 2019. Date referenced: March 4th, 2019).

This dog had a soul, or it would not have done this. *He had to know the child was helpless.*

There have been many cases like these which are too numerous to mention here. All these stories prove that animals have souls by showing unconditional love, reasoning, and the willingness to put their own lives in danger to save a human being.

I have an example of my own too. When we got our Cockatiel Co-Co, Petie didn't like him. He tried to go after Co-Co. Petie's instinct was to chase Co-Co and possibly eat him. Yet, after showing Petie that we loved Co-Co, not only did he leave Co-Co alone, he became his friend and even protected him. They would lay on the couch together and even kiss each other. Co-Co began to feed Petie his bird seed too. This shows a change in thinking, emotions, and the ability to reason. It also shows that he had a soul and that Petie was able to learn to love another fellow creature.

Whether we want to admit it or not, animals are much like us and scientists know this.

> **Scientific Fact/Proof:** *Humans and animals are made of the same biological materials. All the cells of living creatures are the same. Even our DNA is the same, and yet a bit different.*
>
> (Source referenced: Putting DNA to work website: https://www.koshland-science museum.org/sites/all/exhibits/exhibitdna/intro03.jsp. Updated 2019. Referenced source on March 4th, 2019.

The soul/spirit is in our DNA, which is in our blood. The small difference in the DNA is what makes a cat a cat, and a human a human. The DNA in all living creatures is basically the same with some small differences, in the same respect as each person is basically the same, yet different.

Humans and animals all share the same biological components and God loves us all the same; only with a different love for each creature. We animal lovers have a spiritual connection and kinship with animals which allows our souls to bond with an animal's soul. This is one of the reasons we grieve; because we have temporarily lost that spiritual bond. Those who think animals are stupid and worthless do not know this spiritual bond. We have been given a unique spiritual gift that many people do not have.

(All stories above and in this chapter were taken from the website: Animal Wised, by Josie F. Turner: https://www.animalwised.com/top-10-unbelievable-animals-that-saved-people-s-lives-2475.html. Published 2019. Date referenced: March 4th, 2019).

Chapter Eleven

TRUE STORIES OF PEOPLE WHO HAVE SEEN THEIR ANIMALS IN HEAVEN

Now we shall look at people who have had NDE's (Near Death Experiences). This occurs when someone has died for a short period of time and then they come back to life. They claim that they went to Heaven and that they have seen their animals and family members.

Story 1: A woman named Jan had a fatal heart attack and she died for approximately four minutes. She said that she remembers seeing her dead body on the operating table from the location of the ceiling. She states that she saw "beings of light" by her side and that she felt as though she was being raised to a different level of awareness. She then saw her dog Maggi and Maggi appeared in a physical form and looked to be young and healthy. Jan recalls that her dog took her to see her relatives and many other wonderous things. If you notice, she said that *she met her dog first before any humans* and that her dog escorted her around Heaven showing her many wonders.

> (Accessed from the website: Near-Death Experiences and the Afterlife by Kevin R. Williams. https://www.near-death.com/experiences/with-pets.html. C. 2017. Date referenced: March 5th, 2019.)

I can concur with this because when I saw my dogs in Heaven, they were young, vibrant, and healthy.

> *Story 2:* Our second story is about a thirteen-year old child named Lynn. She was undergoing open heart surgery when a problem occurred during the operation and she died. She says that she saw her body on the operating table from the ceiling and then she went through a tunnel and into a bright light. Through this light came two of her dogs that had passed three years prior. One dog's name was Mimi and the other was named Sam. The dogs ran up to her and began kissing her with their tongues, but she said their tongues were not wet. She stated that she felt no weight when the dogs jumped up

on her and the dogs seemed to glow from a light within their bodies. The dogs then led her towards a curtain of colored lights and as she passed through these lights, she saw people as far as her eyes could see and they were all glowing from inside just like her dogs. She further states that she could see fields and hills under an intense blue sky. A voice from the light told her she had to go back, and she asked if her dogs would be here waiting for her when she returned and the voice answered, *"Yes, they will be here waiting for you"*.

> (Accessed from the website: Near-Death Experiences and the Afterlife by Kevin R. Williams. https://www.near-death.com/experiences/with-pets.html. C. 2017. Date referenced: March 5th, 2019.)

When I was in Heaven my dogs kissed me and their kisses were not wet either and they were glowing with a beautiful white light.

Story 3: Our third story concerns the NDE of a woman named Grace. While giving birth there were complications and she died during labor. She said that she passed through a portal that had a peculiar glow to it and that in the blink of an eye she was on the other side of the portal. She says that there was in an intense emerald green light and as the light subsided, she could see beautiful fields with rolling green hills. She said that the sky was an intense blue color that she had never seen before. She saw many of her family members that had passed. And as she looked down, she saw her dog Lucky who had passed when Grace was very young. She claims that she knows her dog will be there waiting for her in Heaven.

> (Accessed from the website: Near-Death Experiences and the Afterlife by Kevin R. Williams. https://www.near-death.com/experiences/with-pets.html. C. 2017. Date referenced: March 5th, 2019.)

I also saw a beautiful field with flowers and colors I had never seen on earth and the sky was a beautiful and intense blue.

Story 4: The next story is about a woman named Susan. She states that she was never a religious person and didn't really believe in God or Heaven. She was anorexic and at the age of twenty-six she weighed 26 lbs. Not long after this she suffered kidney failure and she then turned to God to help her in desperation. She promised God that she would live just for Him if He helped her. While taking dialysis she passed and she states that as soon as she died, she floated upward into Heaven.

She knew it was Heaven because she had never seen or smelled flowers like the ones she saw and that she had never seen so much beauty anywhere as she was seeing at this moment. She then saw her grandmother that had passed many years before and she looked to be thirty years old but had died at the age of seventy. Her grandmother then took her to see Jesus and she said she wept upon seeing Him. She says that Jesus looked at her and she knew she was healed. She then saw every pet that she had ever owned and that they were young and vibrant and that she knew they were waiting for her to return. She said that all the animals had a special caretaker that gave them everything that they needed. Upon Grace's return she was completely healed, gaining back her correct weight and was never anorexic again. All the doctors were stunned at her instant recovery and unable to explain this miracle.

(Accessed from the website: Near-Death Experiences and the Afterlife by Kevin R. Williams. https://www.near-death.com/experiences/with-pets.html. C. 2017. Date referenced: March 5th, 2019.)

I too have had a vision where I was taken to Heaven and I can attest to these people's claims as I have seen and heard many of the same things as they have described while in Heaven. I can assure you as they can; that our animals are in Heaven and they are waiting for our arrival. Your beloved animal is in a place so wonderful, that you cannot even begin to imagine what it is like! Grieve no more. S.W.

(All stories above and in this chapter were taken from the website: Near-Death Experiences and the Afterlife by Kevin R. Williams. https://www.near-death.com/experiences/with-pets.html. C. 2017. Date referenced: March 5th, 2019.)

Chapter Twelve

MY TRIP TO HEAVEN: WHAT I LEARNED ABOUT THE SOUL

First, I would like to take the time to validate the stories in the last chapter. When I was taken to Heaven in my vision, I experienced many of the same things as the people in the stories in the last chapter. I was in a beautiful field and there were purple mountains in the far distance, and I saw colors that I have never seen on this earth. I cannot put a name to the colors of the flowers that were in this field. They were very beautiful, with the most intense colors that I have ever seen. The flowers had a fragrance unknown to me, and the smell seemed to invigorate my whole being. They were swaying back and forth, and they seemed to be singing, or humming. The sky was beautiful with an intense blue and as it stretched far away into the distance, it faded to purple. The clouds were puffy with a completely different texture than those on earth. I saw trees in the distance, and they were swaying; but there was no wind. I knew that the flowers and the trees were alive.

When I saw my dogs, they were young and vibrant, and they glowed with a white light. I knew the glow was from the intensity of their overpowering love and their eternal spirit; which I knew was coming from Jesus because He had the same glow. My dogs (licked) kissed me too and their kisses were not wet. All three of my dogs had big eyes and they talked to me, but they did not use their mouths. We talked with our thoughts, and this seemed more of a *personal* communication than using our mouths to talk. I knew this form of communication was coming from our souls. I too, was told that my dogs would be in Heaven waiting for me. If you would like to read my entire vision and what I learned, please refer to my first and second books.

Now let's unveil the mystery and the truth about the soul. First, we must understand that our bodies are *earthly,* and that they die and decay, but our souls are *spiritual,* and they live for eternity; and this includes the souls of animals. Remember; everything that is alive is energy.

The best analogy I can think of to help you understand the spirit and the soul is this: Let's suppose the soul is the automobile and the spirit is the fuel (gas). A car can go fast, slow, forward, backward, stop, go, turn, and most importantly, *it can take you to a destination.* However, the car can't do anything without the gas, and when a creature dies, the spirit (energy) *takes the soul to its destination*; which is Heaven. Remember in an earlier chapter, we saw that Science and the Bible both agree that energy *transfers*. The spirit/soul *(or energy)* of all living creatures, including animals, go *(transfer)* to Heaven.

God breaths His energy or spirit, into the bodies of humans and animals by His breath; transferring His energy into us. What blooms, evolves, grows, or develops out of this energy is our soul, our personality; all our feelings, thoughts, and actions come from the soul.

Jesus Himself tells us that the spirit *(energy)* takes the soul to Heaven in this next verse:

> *"And when Je'-sus had cried with a loud voice, he said, Father, into thy hands I commend my spirit: and having said thus, he gave up the ghost." (Luke 23:46)*

Jesus commends His spirit to God, knowing that God will take His spirit to Heaven, and knowing also that His soul will go with it. In this verse, Luke also states the fact that the spirit took the soul of Jesus to Heaven when he says, *"...he gave up the ghost..."*. He was talking about the Holy Ghost, or as many people call it, the *Holy Spirit*. The energy, or spirit that God gives all creatures is not just a spirit, it is a *holy spirit*. We humans mar it with sin, but animals are sinless and pure.

King David commits his spirit, into the hands of God because he knows that all spirits and souls go to Heaven into the hands of God, which we know is Heaven.

> *"Into thine hand I commit my spirit: thou hast redeemed me, O Lord God of truth." (Psalm 31:5)*

I have heard many people say that when their pet passes, they feel as though a piece of their soul has been taken from their bodies. They were right, it has. When we bond with our animals, we actually meld with their soul, and we become spiritually one with our animal.

> Webster's definition of the word bond means: *Something that binds and fastens; To join.* (Page 152)

Our soul and our animal's soul actually become one here on earth. When our beloved animal passes, that spiritual bond is broken, and this is what causes much of our pain. To put it bluntly, their soul is ripped from our soul and we feel it down deep, and we don't understand what has happened. They have gone to the spirit world and we are still earthbound. But the good news is that in Heaven, through our love, we will bond again with our animals, and it is a bond that is a thousand times stronger and more beautiful than here in this corrupt world, and it will be forever. Take heart, you will be with your animal in eternity, and you and your animal will have eternal bodies that will never part again. You will be with all of your animals when you enter into eternity.

Ten-Step Program To Recovery Key Points To Remember

Now that you have read this book, I would like to summarize the key points to recovery. If negative feelings come back, you can read this book again, or you can refer to these key points and use this Ten-Step Program.

1. Remind yourself that guilt feelings have no place in your mind. You gave all the love you could give to your pet and you also *saved* a life by giving your recently deceased pet a safe and loving home. Give yourself credit for saving an animal and think of only the good memories. Saving an animal makes you a hero and know that God is proud of you for taking care of His animal.
2. Scientists and the Bible both agree that energy/souls don't die; and we know that animals have souls.

3. Animals have souls and they do go to Heaven. When you meet your beloved pet in the afterlife, it will be forever. Your souls will be fully bonded never to part again.
4. Remember that your beloved animal is in Heaven. Your pet is waiting for you in a place that is so great we can't even begin to imagine it.
5. Do not talk to people who don't understand. Talk with only people who know how you feel. Join a pet loss support group on-line. Do something that makes you feel good; adopting again or donating to a local shelter helps.
6. Have a funeral and place a headstone where you can visit frequently. Put a picture of your animal in the rooms you frequent the most.
7. Adopt another animal when you feel ready. There is nothing more medicinal than loving another animal. Your pet that has passed will not be mad or jealous; they will be honored and happy that you saved another animal and so will God, and there will be one more animal to greet you in Heaven.
8. Remember that the time you had with your beloved pet was well worth the pain of loss and know that *you will see them again*.
9. The fact is; animals have a much shorter life span than humans. Perhaps because God wants you to have many animals waiting for you in Heaven.

10. Know that the love for your departed pet was not wasted, because that very love will unite and bond you with your beloved animal in Heaven. Don't waste your special gift of unconditional love by not loving. There are many animals that are searching for love, just like you. Save another animal.

About the Author

Steven Woodward was born in Houston, Texas and has lived in several states in the south but now resides in West Virginia with his wife, two sons, and four grandchildren.

He enjoys hobbies such as playing guitar, harmonica, and the banjo. Steven spent four years in the United States Navy as a Communications Technician and graduated from Shepherd University in 2001 with a Psychology degree; graduating with full honors at the age of 40 and was inducted into two Honor Societies.

Steven has published two pieces of literature in the Sans Merci at Shepherd University and has published three books on pet loss and animal abuse awareness. Steven has worked as a psychologist/counselor in the field of substance abuse and family counseling.

He is the father of two wonderful sons and has four precious grandchildren. Steven has a Cairn Terrier named Jasper and he is spoiled rotten.

Other Books by Steven Woodward Books for Pet Loss and Proof of the Afterlife for Animals

"Biblical Proof Animals Do Go To Heaven" By Steven H. Woodward, (2012).

When Steven lost his beloved dog BJ he was devastated. Steven had to know if BJ was in heaven or just a pile of dust. After much praying Steven was given a vision where he was taken to Heaven to see BJ along with all his other dogs. Read of his vision and all the proof that he was given that prove animals have souls and do go to Heaven. A book for pet loss.

"God's Revelations Of Animals And People" By Steven H. Woodward, (2017).

Seven years after writing his first book, Steven was given many more revelations of proof that animals do go to Heaven.

His second book contains much more proof, and some of his personal visions (including the vision of BJ), and answers to questions that people have asked him about his first book regarding what he saw in Heaven. Also, in this book Steven dispels several myths about the Bible and reveals several secrets of the Bible. A book for pet loss.

"BJ: A Dog's Journey Into The Afterlife" By Steven H. Woodward, (2018).

This is a beautiful story of the afterlife. It is a story of fiction based on *true events* that happened to Steven and his dog BJ which he writes about in his first book. But this story is told by BJ; through his eyes. In this story BJ has a near death experience and goes to Heaven but he is sent back to life on a mission; he must come back to earth and save a man he has never met. BJ is street wise and he doesn't care much for humans, but he is determined to complete his mission. This story is about BJ's journey to find this mystery man and unconditional love. Steven has endeavored to tell this story inside the mind of his dog BJ, using BJ's unique personality and character. A great book that helps people to understand how animals think and feel; which is much like us. A book that teaches young children how precious animals really are. A book for all ages. A book for pet loss.

Visit Steven Woodward's Facebook Page at: Steven Woodward or visit this link: https://www.facebook.com/profile.php?id=100010267894532

Steven Woodward's books can be purchased at amazon.com or barnesandnoble.com and many other web sites.
All books available in Book and Kindle.

Work Cited

*King James Version of the Holy Bible. Large Compact Edition. Published by Holman Bible Publishers, Nashville Tennessee. Copyright 1998. Mass Market Edition 005405430

*Random House Webster's College Dictionary. Copyright 2000 by Random House, Inc. April 2000 Second Revised.

Works sited/bibliography - INTERNET SOURCES REFERENCED:

* https://www.animalfacts.net/ Animals facts website. C. 2008 – 2019. Date accessed: March 2nd, 2019.

* OSHO website: c. 2019. Date accessed; March 3rd. https://www.osho.com/meditate/meditation-tool-kit/questions-about-meditation/what-is-the-relationship-between-consciousness-and-energy

* Medical News Today website: Published on June 2, 2017. https://www.scientificstyleandformat.org/Tools/SSF-Citation-Quick-Guide.html. Date accessed: March 3rd, 2019.

*Medical News Today website: Published on June 2, 2017. https://www.scientificstyleandformat.org/Tools/SSF-Citation-Quick-Guide.html. Date accessed: March 3rd, 2019.

*All You Need is Biology website: https://allyouneedisbiology.wordpress.com/2016/04/09/play-in-animals/. C. 2016. Date accessed: March 3rd, 2019

*National Geographic website: https://news.nationalgeographic.com/2015/07/150714-animal-dog-thinking-feelings-brain-science/. *C. 2019*. Date accessed: March 4th, 2019.

*Life Wellness website by Carolyn Gregoire. https://www.huffpost.com/entry/proof-that-animals-are-wa_n_4255262?guccounter=1. Updated Dec. 7, 2017. Date accessed: March 4th, 2019.

*The Atlantic website. https://www.theatlantic.com/magazine/archive/2015/04/the-science-of-near-death-experiences/386231/. C. April 2016. Date accessed: March 4th, 2019.

Billy Graham Association website. https://psychcentral.com/lib/grieving-the-loss-of-a-pet/ by Julie Axelrod. Last update: 8 Oct.,2018. Date accessed: March 4th, 2019.

*Putting DNA to work website: https://www.koshland-science museum.org/sites/all/exhibits/exhibitdna/intro03.jsp. Updated 2019. Date accessed: March 4th, 2019.

*Animal Wised, by Josie F. Turner: https://www.animalwised.com/top-10-unbelievable-animals-that-saved-people-s-lives-2475.html. Published 2019. Date accessed: March 4th, 2019.

*Near-Death Experiences and the Afterlife by Kevin R. Williams. https://www.near-death.com/experiences/with-pets.html. C. 2017. Date accessed: March 5th, 2019.

Ten-Step Recovery Program created by Steven H. Woodward.

www.ingramcontent.com/pod-product-compliance
Ingram Content Group UK Ltd.
Pitfield, Milton Keynes, MK11 3LW, UK
UKHW022222230426
12048UKWH00016BA/1008